CW00504456

PHRASEBOOK

— LATVIAN —

THE MOST IMPORTANT PHRASES

This phrasebook contains the most important phrases and questions for basic communication
Everything you need to survive overseas

By Andrey Taranov

T&P BOOKS

...rasebook   ...tionary

English-Latvian phrasebook & mini dictionary

By Andrey Taranov

The collection of "Everything Will Be Okay" travel phrasebooks published by T&P Books is designed for people traveling abroad for tourism and business. The phrasebooks contain what matters most - the essentials for basic communication. This is an indispensable set of phrases to "survive" while abroad.

You'll also find a mini dictionary with 250 useful words required for everyday communication - the names of months and days of the week, measurements, family members, and more.

T&P Books Publishing
www.tpbooks.com

ISBN: 978-1-78716-258-7

This book is also available in E-book formats.
Please visit www.tpbooks.com or the major online bookstores.

FOREWORD

The collection of "Everything Will Be Okay" travel phrasebooks published by T&P Books is designed for people traveling abroad for tourism and business. The phrasebooks contain what matters most - the essentials for basic communication. This is an indispensable set of phrases to "survive" while abroad.

This phrasebook will help you in most cases where you need to ask something, get directions, find out how much something costs, etc. It can also resolve difficult communication situations where gestures just won't help.

This book contains a lot of phrases that have been grouped according to the most relevant topics. You'll also find a mini dictionary with useful words - numbers, time, calendar, colors...

Take "Everything Will Be Okay" phrasebook with you on the road and you'll have an irreplaceable traveling companion who will help you find your way out of any situation and teach you to not fear speaking with foreigners.

TABLE OF CONTENTS

T&P Books Publishing

LIST OF ABBREVIATIONS

English abbreviations

ab.	-	about
adj	-	adjective
adv	-	adverb
anim.	-	animate
as adj	-	attributive noun used as adjective
e.g.	-	for example
etc.	-	et cetera
fam.	-	familiar
fem.	-	feminine
form.	-	formal
inanim.	-	inanimate
masc.	-	masculine
math	-	mathematics
mil.	-	military
n	-	noun
pl	-	plural
pron.	-	pronoun
sb	-	somebody
sing.	-	singular
sth	-	something
v aux	-	auxiliary verb
vi	-	intransitive verb
vi, vt	-	intransitive, transitive verb
vt	-	transitive verb

Latvian abbreviations

s	-	feminine noun
s dsk	-	feminine plural
s, v	-	masculine, feminine
v	-	masculine noun
v dsk	-	masculine plural

LATVIAN
PHRASEBOOK

This section contains
important phrases that may
come in handy in various
real-life situations.
The phrasebook will help
you ask for directions, clarify
a price, buy tickets, and
order food at a restaurant

T&P Books Publishing

PHRASEBOOK
CONTENTS

T&P Books Publishing

The bare minimum

Excuse me, ...	**Atvainojiet, ...** [atvainɔjiɛt, ...]
Hello.	**Sveicināti.** [svɛitsina:ti.]
Thank you.	**Paldies.** [paldiɛs.]
Good bye.	**Uz redzēšanos.** [uz redze:ʃanɔs.]
Yes.	**Jā.** [ja:.]
No.	**Nē.** [ne:.]
I don't know.	**Es nezinu.** [es nezinu.]
Where? | Where to? | When?	**Kur? | Uz kurieni? | Kad?** [kur? | uz kuriɛni? | kad?]

I need ...	**Man vajag ...** [man vajag ...]
I want ...	**Es gribu ...** [es gribu ...]
Do you have ...?	**Vai jums ir ...?** [vai jums ir ...?]
Is there a ... here?	**Vai šeit ir ...?** [vai ʃɛit ir ...?]
May I ...?	**Vai drīkstu ...?** [vai dri:kstu ...?]
..., please (polite request)	**Lūdzu, ...** [lu:dzu, ...]

I'm looking for ...	**Es meklēju ...** [es mekle:ju ...]
restroom	**tualeti** [tualeti]
ATM	**bankomātu** [bankɔma:tu]
pharmacy (drugstore)	**aptieku** [aptiɛku]
hospital	**slimnīcu** [slimni:tsu]
police station	**policijas iecirkni** [pɔlitsi:jas iɛtsirkni]
subway	**metro** [metrɔ]

taxi	**taksometru** [taksɔmetru]
train station	**dzelzceļa staciju** [dzelztsɛl'a statsiju]

My name is …	**Mani sauc …** [mani sauts …]
What's your name?	**Kā jūs sauc?** [ka: ju:s sauts?]
Could you please help me?	**Lūdzu, palīdziet.** [lu:dzu, pali:dziɛt.]
I've got a problem.	**Man ir problēma.** [man ir prɔblɛ:ma.]
I don't feel well.	**Man ir slikti.** [man ir slikti.]
Call an ambulance!	**Izsauciet ātro palīdzību!** [izsautsiɛt a:trɔ pali:dzi:bu!]
May I make a call?	**Vai drīkstu piezvanīt?** [vai dri:kstu piɛzvani:t?]

I'm sorry.	**Atvainojos.** [atvainɔjɔs.]
You're welcome.	**Lūdzu.** [lu:dzu.]

I, me	**es** [es]
you (inform.)	**tu** [tu]
he	**viņš** [viɲʃ]
she	**viņa** [viɲa]
they (masc.)	**viņi** [viɲi]
they (fem.)	**viņas** [viɲas]
we	**mēs** [me:s]
you (pl)	**jūs** [ju:s]
you (sg, form.)	**Jūs** [ju:s]

ENTRANCE	**IEEJA** [iɛeja]
EXIT	**IZEJA** [izeja]
OUT OF ORDER	**NESTRĀDĀ** [nestra:da:]
CLOSED	**SLĒGTS** [sle:gts]

OPEN	**ATVĒRTS** [atve:rts]
FOR WOMEN	**SIEVIETĒM** [siɛviɛte:m]
FOR MEN	**VĪRIEŠIEM** [vi:riɛʃiɛm]

Questions

Where?	**Kur?** [kur?]
Where to?	**Uz kurieni?** [uz kuriɛni?]
Where from?	**No kurienes?** [nɔ kuriɛnes?]
Why?	**Kāpēc?** [kaːpeːts?]
For what reason?	**Kādēļ?** [kaːdeːlʲ?]
When?	**Kad?** [kad?]

How long?	**Cik ilgi?** [tsik ilgi?]
At what time?	**Cikos?** [tsikɔs?]
How much?	**Cik maksā?** [tsik maksaː?]
Do you have ...?	**Vai jums ir ...?** [vai jums ir ...?]
Where is ...?	**Kur atrodas ...?** [kur atrɔdas ...?]

What time is it?	**Cik pulkstens?** [tsik pulkstens?]
May I make a call?	**Vai drīkstu piezvanīt?** [vai driːkstu piɛzvaniːt?]
Who's there?	**Kas tur ir?** [kas tur ir?]
Can I smoke here?	**Vai te drīkst smēķēt?** [vai te driːkst smɛːtʲeːt?]
May I ...?	**Vai drīkstu ...?** [vai driːkstu ...?]

Needs

I'd like …	**Es gribētu …** [es gribɛ:tu …]
I don't want …	**Es negribu …** [es negribu …]
I'm thirsty.	**Man slāpst.** [man sla:pst.]
I want to sleep.	**Es gribu gulēt.** [es gribu gule:t.]

I want …	**Es gribu …** [es gribu …]
to wash up	**nomazgāties** [nɔmazga:tiɛs]
to brush my teeth	**iztīrīt zobus** [izti:ri:t zɔbus]
to rest a while	**nedaudz atpūsties** [nɛdaudz atpu:stiɛs]
to change my clothes	**pārģērbties** [pa:rdʲe:rbtiɛs]

to go back to the hotel	**atgriezties viesnīcā** [atgriɛzties viɛsni:tsa:]
to buy …	**nopirkt …** [nɔpirkt …]
to go to …	**doties uz …** [dɔties uz …]
to visit …	**apmeklēt …** [apmekle:t …]
to meet with …	**satikties ar …** [satikties ar …]
to make a call	**piezvanīt** [piɛzvani:t]

I'm tired.	**Es esmu noguris /nogurusi/.** [es esmu nɔguris /nɔgurusi/.]
We are tired.	**Mēs esam noguruši /nogurušas/.** [me:s ɛsam nɔguruʃi /nɔguruʃas/.]
I'm cold.	**Man ir auksti.** [man ir auksti.]
I'm hot.	**Man ir karsti.** [man ir karsti.]
I'm OK.	**Man viss kārtībā.** [man vis ka:rti:ba:.]

I need to make a call.

Man jāpiezvana.
[man jaːpiɛzvana.]

I need to go to the restroom.

Man vajag uz tualeti.
[man vajag uz tualeti.]

I have to go.

Man laiks doties.
[man laiks dɔtiɛs.]

I have to go now.

Man jāiet.
[man jaːiɛt.]

Asking for directions

Excuse me, ...	**Atvainojiet, ...** [atvainɔjiɛt, ...]
Where is ...?	**Kur atrodas ...?** [kur atrɔdas ...?]
Which way is ...?	**Kurā virzienā ir ...?** [kura: virziɛna: ir ...?]
Could you help me, please?	**Lūdzu, palīdziet.** [lu:dzu, pali:dziɛt.]
I'm looking for ...	**Es meklēju ...** [es mekle:ju ...]
I'm looking for the exit.	**Es meklēju izeju.** [es mekle:ju izeju.]
I'm going to ...	**Es dodos uz ...** [es dɔdɔs uz ...]
Am I going the right way to ...?	**Vai eju pareizā virzienā ...?** [vai eju parɛiza: virziɛna: ...?]
Is it far?	**Vai tas ir tālu?** [vai tas ir ta:lu?]
Can I get there on foot?	**Vai es aiziešu ar kājām?** [vai es aiziɛʃu ar ka:ja:m?]
Can you show me on the map?	**Lūdzu, parādiet to uz kartes?** [lu:dzu, para:diɛt tɔ uz kartes?]
Show me where we are right now.	**Parādiet, kur mēs tagad atrodamies?** [para:diɛt, kur me:s tagad atrɔdamiɛs?]
Here	**Šeit** [ʃɛit]
There	**Tur** [tur]
This way	**Šurp** [ʃurp]
Turn right.	**Griezieties pa labi.** [griɛziɛties pa labi.]
Turn left.	**Griezieties pa kreisi.** [griɛziɛties pa krɛisi.]
first (second, third) turn	**pirmais (otrais, trešais) pagrieziens** [pirmais pagriɛziɛns]

to the right

pa labi
[pa labi]

to the left

pa kreisi
[pa krɛisi]

Go straight ahead.

Ejiet taisni uz priekšu.
[ejiɛt taisni uz priɛkʃu.]

Signs

WELCOME!	**LAIPNI LŪGTI!** [laipni lu:gti!]
ENTRANCE	**IEEJA** [iɛeja]
EXIT	**IZEJA** [izeja]

PUSH	**GRŪST** [gru:st]
PULL	**VILKT** [vilkt]
OPEN	**ATVĒRTS** [atve:rts]
CLOSED	**AIZVĒRTS** [sle:gts]

FOR WOMEN	**SIEVIETĒM** [siɛviɛte:m]
FOR MEN	**VĪRIEŠIEM** [vi:riɛʃiɛm]
GENTLEMEN, GENTS (m)	**VĪRIEŠU TUALETE** [vi:riɛʃu tualɛte]
WOMEN (f)	**SIEVIEŠU TUALETE** [siɛviɛʃu tualɛte]

DISCOUNTS	**ATLAIDES** [atlaides]
SALE	**IZPĀRDOŠANA** [izpa:rdoʃana]
FREE	**BEZ MAKSAS** [bezmaksas]
NEW!	**JAUNUMS!** [jaunums!]
ATTENTION!	**UZMANĪBU!** [uzmani:bu!]

NO VACANCIES	**BRĪVU VIETU NAV** [bri:vu viɛtu nav]
RESERVED	**REZERVĒTS** [rɛzerve:ts]
ADMINISTRATION	**ADMINISTRĀCIJA** [administra:tsija]
STAFF ONLY	**TIKAI DARBINIEKIEM** [tikai pɛrsɔna:lam]

BEWARE OF THE DOG!	**NIKNS SUNS!** [nikns suns]
NO SMOKING!	**SMĒĶĒT AIZLIEGTS!** [smɛ:tʲe:t aizliɛgts!]
DO NOT TOUCH!	**AR ROKĀM NEAIZTIKT!** [ar rɔka:m neaiztikt!]
DANGEROUS	**BĪSTAMI!** [bi:stami]
DANGER	**BĪSTAMS!** [bi:stams]
HIGH VOLTAGE	**AUGSTSPRIEGUMS!** [augstspriɛgums]
NO SWIMMING!	**PELDĒT AIZLIEGTS!** [pelde:t aizliɛgts!]

OUT OF ORDER	**NESTRĀDĀ** [nestra:da:]
FLAMMABLE	**UGUNSNEDROŠS** [ugunsnedrɔʃs]
FORBIDDEN	**AIZLIEGTS** [aizliɛgts]
NO TRESPASSING!	**IEBRAUKT AIZLIEGTS!** [iɛiɛja aizliɛgta]
WET PAINT	**SVAIGI KRĀSOTS** [svaigi kra:sots]

CLOSED FOR RENOVATIONS	**UZ REMONTA LAIKU SLĒGTS** [uz remɔnta laiku sle:gts]
WORKS AHEAD	**UZ CEĻA STRĀDĀ** [uz tsɛlʲa stra:da:]
DETOUR	**APVEDCEĻŠ** [apvedtselʲʃ]

Transportation. General phrases

plane	**lidmašīna** [lidmaʃi:na]
train	**vilciens** [viltsiɛns]
bus	**autobuss** [autɔbus]
ferry	**prāmis** [pra:mis]
taxi	**taksometrs** [taksɔmetrs]
car	**automašīna** [maʃi:na]
schedule	**saraksts** [saraksts]
Where can I see the schedule?	**Kur var apskatīt sarakstu?** [kur var apskati:t sarakstu?]
workdays (weekdays)	**darba dienas** [darba diɛnas]
weekends	**nedēļas nogales** [nɛdɛ:lʲas nɔgales]
holidays	**svētku dienas** [sve:tku diɛnas]
DEPARTURE	**IZLIDOŠANA** [izlidɔʃana]
ARRIVAL	**IELIDOŠANA** [iɛlidɔʃana]
DELAYED	**KAVĒJAS** [kave:jas]
CANCELLED	**ATCELTS** [attselts]
next (train, etc.)	**nākamais** [na:kamais]
first	**pirmais** [pirmais]
last	**pēdējais** [pɛ:de:jais]
When is the next ...?	**Kad būs nākošais ...?** [kad bu:s na:kɔʃais ...?]
When is the first ...?	**Kad pienāk pirmais ...?** [kad piɛna:k pirmais ...?]

When is the last ...?	**Kad atiet pēdējais ...?** [kad atiɛt pɛ:de:jais ...?]
transfer (change of trains, etc.)	**pārsēšanās** [pa:rse:ʃana:s]
to make a transfer	**pārsēsties** [pa:rse:stiɛs]
Do I need to make a transfer?	**Vai man ir jāpārsēžas?** [vai man ir ja:pa:rse:ʒas?]

Buying tickets

Where can I buy tickets?	**Kur es varu nopirkt biļetes?** [kur es varu nɔpirkt biļʲɛtes?]
ticket	**biļete** [biļʲɛte]
to buy a ticket	**nopirkt biļeti** [nɔpirkt biļʲeti]
ticket price	**biļetes cena** [biļʲɛtes tsɛna]

Where to?	**Uz kurieni?** [uz kuriɛni?]
To what station?	**Līdz kurai stacijai?** [liːdz kurai statsijai?]
I need ...	**Man vajag ...** [man vajag ...]
one ticket	**vienu biļeti** [viɛnu biļʲeti]
two tickets	**divas biļetes** [divas biļʲɛtes]
three tickets	**trīs biļetes** [triːs biļʲɛtes]

one-way	**vienā virzienā** [viɛnaː virziɛnaː]
round-trip	**turp un atpakaļ** [turp un atpakaļʲ]
first class	**pirmā klase** [pirmaː klase]
second class	**otrā klase** [ɔtraː klase]

today	**šodien** [ʃɔdiɛn]
tomorrow	**rīt** [riːt]
the day after tomorrow	**parīt** [pariːt]
in the morning	**no rīta** [nɔ riːta]
in the afternoon	**pēcpusdienā** [peːtspusdiɛnaː]
in the evening	**vakarā** [vakaraː]

aisle seat	**ejas sēdvieta** [ejas se:dvieta]
window seat	**sēdvieta pie loga** [se:dvieta pie loga]
How much?	**Cik maksā?** [tsik maksa:?]
Can I pay by credit card?	**Vai varu samkasāt ar karti?** [vai varu samkasa:t ar karti?]

Bus

bus	**autobuss** [autɔbus]
intercity bus	**starppilsētu autobuss** [starppilsɛ:tu autɔbus]
bus stop	**autobusa pietura** [autɔbusa piɛtura]
Where's the nearest bus stop?	**Kur ir tuvākā autobusa pietura?** [kur ir tuva:ka: autɔbusa piɛtura?]

number (bus ~, etc.)	**numurs** [numurs]
Which bus do I take to get to …?	**Kurš autobus brauc līdz …?** [kurʃ autɔbus brauts li:dz …?]
Does this bus go to …?	**Vai šis autobus brauc līdz …?** [vai ʃis autɔbus brauts li:dz …?]
How frequent are the buses?	**Cik bieži kursē autobusi?** [tsik biɛʒi kurse: autɔbusi?]

every 15 minutes	**katras piecpadsmit minūtes** [katras piɛtspadsmit minu:tes]
every half hour	**katru pusstundu** [katru pustundu]
every hour	**katru stundu** [katru stundu]
several times a day	**vairākas reizes dienā** [vaira:kas rɛizes diɛna:]
… times a day	**… reizes dienā** [… rɛizes diɛna:]

schedule	**saraksts** [saraksts]
Where can I see the schedule?	**Kur var apskatīt sarakstu?** [kur var apskati:t sarakstu?]
When is the next bus?	**Kad būs nākošais autobuss?** [kad bu:s na:kɔʃais autɔbus?]
When is the first bus?	**Kad pienāk pirmais autobuss?** [kad piɛna:k pirmais autɔbus?]
When is the last bus?	**Kad atiet pēdējais autobuss?** [kad atiɛt pɛ:de:jais autɔbus?]

stop	**pietura** [piɛtura]
next stop	**nākošā pietura** [na:kama: piɛtura]

last stop (terminus)

gala pietura
[gala piɛtura]

Stop here, please.

Lūdzu, pieturiet šeit.
[lu:dzu, piɛturiɛt ʃɛit.]

Excuse me, this is my stop.

Atvainojiet, šī ir mana pietura.
[atvainɔjiɛt, ʃi: ir mana piɛtura.]

Train

train	vilciens
	[viltsiɛns]
suburban train	priekšpilsētas vilciens
	[priɛkʃpilsɛ:tas viltsiɛns]
long-distance train	tālsatiksmes vilciens
	[ta:lsatiksmes viltsiɛns]
train station	dzelzceļa stacija
	[dzelztsɛlʲa statsija]
Excuse me, where is the exit	Atvainojiet, kur ir izeja uz peronu?
to the platform?	[atvainɔjiɛt, kur ir izeja uz perɔnu?]

Does this train go to ...?	Vai šis vilciens dodas uz ...?
	[vai ʃis viltsiɛns dɔdas uz ...?]
next train	nākošais vilciens
	[na:kɔʃais viltsiɛns]
When is the next train?	Kad pienāks nākošais vilciens?
	[kad piɛna:ks na:kɔʃais viltsiɛns?]
Where can I see the schedule?	Kur var apskatīt sarakstu?
	[kur var apskati:t sarakstu?]
From which platform?	No kura perona?
	[nɔ kura perɔna?]
When does the train arrive in ...?	Kad vilciens pienāk ...?
	[kad viltsiɛns piɛna:k ...?]

Please help me.	Lūdzu, palīdziet.
	[lu:dzu, pali:dziɛt.]
I'm looking for my seat.	Es meklēju savu vietu.
	[es mekle:ju savu viɛtu.]
We're looking for our seats.	Mēs meklējam savas vietas.
	[me:s mekle:jam savas viɛtas.]
My seat is taken.	Mana vieta ir aizņemta.
	[mana viɛta ir aizɲemta.]
Our seats are taken.	Mūsu vietas ir aizņemtas.
	[mu:su viɛtas ir aizɲemtas.]

I'm sorry but this is my seat.	Atvainojiet, bet šī ir mana vieta.
	[atvainɔjiɛt, bet ʃi: ir mana viɛta.]
Is this seat taken?	Vai šī vieta ir aizņemta?
	[vai ʃi: viɛta ir aizɲemta?]
May I sit here?	Vai drīkstu šeit apsēsties?
	[vai dri:kstu ʃɛit apse:stiɛs?]

On the train. Dialogue (No ticket)

Ticket, please.

Jūsu biļeti, lūdzu.
[ju:su biļeti, lu:dzu.]

I don't have a ticket.

Man nav biļetes.
[man nav biļɛtes.]

I lost my ticket.

Es pazaudēju savu biļeti.
[es pazaude:ju savu biļeti.]

I forgot my ticket at home.

Es aizmirsu savu biļeti mājās.
[es aizmirsu savu biļeti ma:ja:s.]

You can buy a ticket from me.

Jūs varat nopirkt biļeti pie manis.
[ju:s varat nopirkt biļeti piɛ manis.]

You will also have to pay a fine.

Jums būs jāsamaksā arī soda nauda.
[jums bu:s ja:samaksa: ari: soda nauda.]

Okay.

Labi.
[labi.]

Where are you going?

Uz kurieni jūs brauciet?
[uz kuriɛni ju:s brautsiɛt?]

I'm going to ...

Es braucu līdz ...
[es brautsu li:dz ...]

How much? I don't understand.

Cik? Es nesaprotu.
[tsik? es nɛsaprotu.]

Write it down, please.

Lūdzu, uzrakstiet to.
[lu:dzu, uzrakstiɛt to.]

Okay. Can I pay with a credit card?

Labi. Vai es varu samaksāt ar karti?
[labi. vai es varu samaksa:t ar karti?]

Yes, you can.

Jā, variet.
[ja:, variɛt.]

Here's your receipt.

Lūdzu, jūsu kvīts.
[lu:dzu, ju:su kvi:ts.]

Sorry about the fine.

Atvainojiet par naudas sodu.
[atvainojiɛt par naudas sodu.]

That's okay. It was my fault.

Tas nekas. Tā bija mana vaina.
[tas nɛkas. ta: bija mana vaina.]

Enjoy your trip.

Patīkamu braucienu.
[pati:kamu brautsiɛnu.]

Taxi

taxi	**taksometrs** [taksɔmetrs]
taxi driver	**taksometra vadītājs** [taksɔmetra vadi:ta:js]
to catch a taxi	**noķert taksometru** [nɔtʲert taksɔmetru]
taxi stand	**taksometra pietura** [taksɔmetra piɛtura]
Where can I get a taxi?	**Kur es varu dabūt taksometru?** [kur ɛs varu dabu:t taksɔmetru?]
to call a taxi	**izsaukt taksometru** [izsaukt taksɔmetru]
I need a taxi.	**Man vajag taksometru.** [man vajag taksɔmetru.]
Right now.	**Tieši tagad.** [tiɛʃi tagad.]
What is your address (location)?	**Jūsu adrese?** [ju:su adrɛse?]
My address is …	**Mana adrese ir …** [mana adrɛse ir …]
Your destination?	**Uz kurieni jūs brauksiet?** [uz kuriɛni ju:s brauksiɛt?]
Excuse me, …	**Atvainojiet, …** [atvainɔjiɛt, …]
Are you available?	**Vai jūs esat brīvs?** [vai ju:s ɛsat bri:vs?]
How much is it to get to …?	**Cik maksā aizbraukt līdz …?** [tsik maksa: aizbraukt li:dz …?]
Do you know where it is?	**Vai jūs zināt, kur tas atrodas?** [vai ju:s zina:t, kur tas atrɔdas?]
Airport, please.	**Līdz lidosta, lūdzu.** [li:dz lidɔsta, lu:dzu.]
Stop here, please.	**Apturiet šeit, lūdzu.** [apturiɛt ʃeit, lu:dzu.]
It's not here.	**Tas nav šeit.** [tas nav ʃɛit.]
This is the wrong address.	**Šī nav pareizā adrese.** [ʃi: nav parɛiza: adrɛse.]
Turn left.	**Tagad pa kreisi.** [tagad pa krɛisi.]
Turn right.	**Tagad pa labi.** [tagad pa labi.]

How much do I owe you?

I'd like a receipt, please.

Keep the change.

Cik esmu jums parādā?
[tsik esmu jums para:da:?]
Es vēlētos čeku, lūdzu.
[es vɛ:le:tɔs tʃɛku, lu:dzu.]
Paturiet atlikumu.
[paturiɛt atlikumu.]

Would you please wait for me?

five minutes

ten minutes

fifteen minutes

twenty minutes

half an hour

Uzgaidiet, lūdzu.
[uzgaidiɛt, lu:dzu.]
piecas minūtes
[piɛtsas minu:tes]
desmit minūtes
[desmit minu:tes]
piecpadsmit minūtes
[piɛtspadsmit minu:tes]
divdesmit minūtes
[divdesmit minu:tes]
pusstundu
[pustundu]

Hotel

Hello.	**Sveicināti.** [svɛitsinaːti.]
My name is …	**Mani sauc …** [mani sauts …]
I have a reservation.	**Man ir rezervēts numurs.** [man ir rɛzerveːts numurs.]
I need …	**Man vajag …** [man vajag …]
a single room	**vienvietīgu numuru** [viɛnviɛtiːgu numuru]
a double room	**divvietīgu numuru** [divviɛtiːgu numuru]
How much is that?	**Cik tas maksā?** [tsik tas maksaː?]
That's a bit expensive.	**Tas ir nedaudz par dārgu.** [tas ir nɛdaudz par daːrgu.]
Do you have anything else?	**Vai jums ir vēl kaut kas?** [vai jums ir veːl kaut kas?]
I'll take it.	**Es to ņemšu.** [es tɔ ɲemʃu.]
I'll pay in cash.	**Es maksāšu skaidrā naudā.** [es maksaːʃu skaidraː naudaː.]
I've got a problem.	**Man ir problēma.** [man ir prɔblɛːma.]
My … is broken.	**Mans /mana/ … ir saplīsis /saplīsusi/.** [mans /mana/ … ir sapliːsis /sapliːsusi/.]
My … is out of order.	**Mans /mana/ … nestrādā.** [mans /mana/ … nestraːdaː.]
TV	**televīzors** [tɛleviːzɔrs]
air conditioner	**gaisa kondicionieris** [gaisa kɔnditsiɔniɛris]
tap	**krāns** [kraːns]
shower	**duša** [duʃa]
sink	**izlietne** [izliɛtne]
safe	**seifs** [sɛifs]

door lock	**slēdzene** [sle:dzɛne]
electrical outlet	**rozete** [rɔzɛte]
hairdryer	**fēns** [fe:ns]

I don't have ...	**Man nav ...** [man nav ...]
water	**ūdens** [u:dens]
light	**gaismas** [gaismas]
electricity	**elektrības** [ɛlektri:bas]

Can you give me ...?	**Vai variet man iedot ...?** [vai variɛt man iɛdɔt ...?]
a towel	**dvieli** [dviɛli]
a blanket	**segu** [sɛgu]
slippers	**čības** [tʃi:bas]
a robe	**halātu** [xala:tu]
shampoo	**šampūnu** [ʃampu:nu]
soap	**ziepes** [ziɛpes]

I'd like to change rooms.	**Es vēlos mainīt numuru.** [es ve:lɔs maini:t numuru.]
I can't find my key.	**Es nevaru atrast savas atslēgas.** [es nɛvaru atrast savas atslɛ:gas.]
Could you open my room, please?	**Vai variet atvērt manu numuru, lūdzu.** [vai variɛt atve:rt manu numuru, lu:dzu.]
Who's there?	**Kas tur ir?** [kas tur ir?]
Come in!	**Ienāciet!** [iɛna:tsiɛt!]
Just a minute!	**Vienu minūti!** [viɛnu minu:ti!]
Not right now, please.	**Lūdzu, ne tagad.** [lu:dzu, ne tagad.]

Come to my room, please.	**Ienāciet pie manis, lūdzu.** [iɛna:tsiɛt piɛ manis, lu:dzu.]
I'd like to order food service.	**Es vēlos pasūtīt ēdienu numurā.** [es ve:lɔs pasu:ti:t e:diɛnu numura:.]
My room number is ...	**Mans istabas numurs ir ...** [mans istabas numurs ir ...]

I'm leaving ...	**Es aizbraucu ...** [es aizbrautsu ...]
We're leaving ...	**Mēs aizbraucam ...** [me:s aizbrautsam ...]
right now	**tagad** [tagad]
this afternoon	**šo pēcpusdien** [ʃɔ pe:tspusdiɛn]
tonight	**šovakar** [ʃɔvakar]
tomorrow	**rīt** [ri:t]
tomorrow morning	**rīt no rīta** [ri:t nɔ ri:ta]
tomorrow evening	**rītvakar** [ri:tvakar]
the day after tomorrow	**parīt** [pari:t]

I'd like to pay.	**Es vēlos norēķināties.** [es ve:lɔs nɔre:tʲina:tiɛs.]
Everything was wonderful.	**Viss bija lieliski.** [vis bija liɛliski.]
Where can I get a taxi?	**Kur es varu dabūt taksometru?** [kur es varu dabu:t taksɔmetru?]
Would you call a taxi for me, please?	**Lūdzu, izsauciet man man taksometru?** [lu:dzu, izsautsiɛt man man taksɔmetru?]

Restaurant

Can I look at the menu, please?

Vai varu apskatīt ēdienkarti?
[vai varu apskati:t e:diɛnkarti?]

Table for one.

Galdiņu vienam.
[galdiɲu viɛnam.]

There are two (three, four) of us.

Mēs esam divi (trīs, četri)
[me:s ɛsam divi]

Smoking

Smēķētājiem
[smɛ:tʲɛ:ta:jiɛm]

No smoking

Nesmēķētājiem
[nesmɛ:tʲɛ:ta:jiɛm]

Excuse me! (addressing a waiter)

Atvainojiet!
[atvainɔjiɛt!]

menu

ēdienkarte
[e:diɛnkarte]

wine list

vīna karte
[vi:na karte]

The menu, please.

Ēdienkarti, lūdzu.
[e:diɛnkarti, lu:dzu.]

Are you ready to order?

Vai esat gatavi pasūtīt?
[vai ɛsat gatavi pasu:ti:t?]

What will you have?

Ko pasūtīsiet?
[kɔ pasu:ti:siɛt?]

I'll have ...

Man ...
[man ...]

I'm a vegetarian.

Es esmu veģetārietis /veģetāriete/ ...
[es esmu vɛdʲɛta:riɛtis /vɛdʲɛta:riɛte/ ...]

meat

gaļa
[galʲa]

fish

zivs
[zivs]

vegetables

dārzeņi
[da:rzeɲi]

Do you have vegetarian dishes?

Vai jums ir veģetārie ēdieni?
[vai jums ir vɛdʲɛta:riɛ e:diɛni?]

I don't eat pork.

Es neēdu cūkgaļu.
[es neɛ:du tsu:kgalʲu.]

He /she/ doesn't eat meat.

Viņš /viņa/ neēd gaļu.
[viɲʃ /viɲa/ nee:d galʲu.]

I am allergic to ...

Man ir alerģija pret ...
[man ir alerdʲija pret ...]

Would you please bring me ...	**Vai, atnesīsiet man ..., lūdzu?** [vai, atnesi:siɛt man ..., lu:dzu?]
salt | pepper | sugar	**sāls | pipari | cukurs** [sa:ls | pipari | tsukurs]
coffee | tea | dessert	**kafija | tēja | deserts** [kafija | te:ja | dɛserts]
water | sparkling | plain	**ūdens | gāzēts | negāzēts** [u:dens | ga:ze:ts | nɛga:ze:ts]
a spoon | fork | knife	**karote | dakša | nazis** [karɔte | dakʃa | nazis]
a plate | napkin	**šķīvis | salvete** [ʃcʲi:vis | salvɛte]

Enjoy your meal!	**Labu apetīti!** [labu apeti:ti!]
One more, please.	**Atnesiet vēl, lūdzu.** [atnesiɛt ve:l, lu:dzu.]
It was very delicious.	**Bija ļoti garšīgi.** [bija lʲɔti garʃi:gi.]

check | change | tip	**čeks | atlikums | dzeramnauda** [re:tʲins | atlikums | dzɛramnauda]
Check, please. (Could I have the check, please?)	**Rēķinu, lūdzu.** [re:tʲinu, lu:dzu.]
Can I pay by credit card?	**Vai varu samaksāt ar karti?** [vai varu samaksa:t ar karti?]
I'm sorry, there's a mistake here.	**Atvainojiet, šeit ir kļūda.** [atvainɔjiɛt, ʃeit ir klʲu:da.]

Shopping

Can I help you?

Kā es varu jums palīdzēt?
[ka: es varu jums pali:dze:t?]

Do you have ...?

Vai jums ir ...?
[vai jums ir ...?]

I'm looking for ...

Es meklēju ...
[es mekle:ju ...]

I need ...

Man vajag ...
[man vajag ...]

I'm just looking.

Es tikai skatos.
[es tikai skatɔs.]

We're just looking.

Mēs tikai skatāmies.
[me:s tikai skata:miɛs.]

I'll come back later.

Es ienākšu vēlāk.
[es iɛna:kʃu vɛ:la:k.]

We'll come back later.

Mēs ienāksim vēlāk.
[me:s iɛna:ksim vɛ:la:k.]

discounts | sale

atlaides | izpārdošana
[atlaides | izpa:rdɔʃana]

Would you please show me ...

Vai parādīsiet man, lūdzu, ...
[vai para:di:siɛt man, lu:dzu, ...]

Would you please give me ...

Vai iedosiet man, lūdzu, ...
[vai iɛdɔsiɛt man, lu:dzu, ...]

Can I try it on?

Vai drīkstu pielaikot?
[vai dri:kstu piɛlaikɔt?]

Excuse me, where's the fitting room?

Atvainojiet, kur ir pielaikošanas kabīne?
[atvainɔjiɛt, kur ir piɛlaikɔʃanas kabi:ne?]

Which color would you like?

Kādu krāsu vēlaties?
[ka:du kra:su vɛ:latiɛs?]

size | length

izmērs | augums
[izmɛ:rs | augums]

How does it fit?

Vai der?
[vai der?]

How much is it?

Cik tas maksā?
[tsik tas maksa:?]

That's too expensive.

Tas ir par dārgu.
[tas ir par da:rgu.]

I'll take it.

Es to ņemšu.
[es tɔ ɲemʃu.]

Excuse me, where do I pay?

Atvainojiet, kur es varu samaksāt?
[atvainɔjiɛt, kur es varu samaksa:t?]

Will you pay in cash or credit card?

**Vai maksāsiet skaidrā naudā
vai ar karti?**
[vai maksa:siɛt skaidra: nauda:
vai ar karti?]

In cash | with credit card

Skaidrā naudā | ar karti
[skaidra: nauda: | ar karti]

Do you want the receipt?

Vai jums vajag čeku?
[vai jums vajag tʃɛku?]

Yes, please.

Jā, lūdzu.
[ja:, lu:dzu.]

No, it's OK.

Nē, paldies.
[ne:, paldiɛs.]

Thank you. Have a nice day!

Paldies. Visu labu!
[paldiɛs. visu labu!]

In town

Excuse me, please.	**Atvainojiet, lūdzu ...** [atvainɔjiɛt, lu:dzu ...]
I'm looking for ...	**Es meklēju ...** [es mekle:ju ...]

the subway	**metro** [metrɔ]
my hotel	**savu viesnīcu** [savu viɛsni:tsu]
the movie theater	**kinoteātri** [kinɔtea:tri]
a taxi stand	**taksometra pieturu** [taksɔmetra piɛturu]

an ATM	**bankomātu** [bankɔma:tu]
a foreign exchange office	**valūtas maiņas punktu** [valu:tas maiɲas punktu]
an internet café	**interneta kafejnīcu** [interneta kafejni:tsu]
... street	**... ielu** [... iɛlu]
this place	**šo vietu** [ʃɔ viɛtu]

Do you know where ... is?	**Vai jūs ziniet, kur atrodas ...?** [vai ju:s ziniɛt, kur atrɔdas ...?]
Which street is this?	**Kā sauc šo ielu?** [ka: sauts ʃɔ iɛlu?]

Show me where we are right now.	**Parādiet, kur mēs tagad atrodamies?** [para:diɛt, kur me:s tagad atrɔdamiɛs?]
Can I get there on foot?	**Vai es aiziešu ar kājām?** [vai es aiziɛʃu ar ka:ja:m?]
Do you have a map of the city?	**Vai jums ir šīs pilsētas karte?** [vai jums ir ʃi:s pilsɛ:tas karte?]

How much is a ticket to get in?	**Cik maksā ieejas biļete?** [tsik maksa: iɛejas biļɛte?]
Can I take pictures here?	**Vai šeit drīkst fotografēt?** [vai ʃɛit dri:kst fotografe:t?]
Are you open?	**Vai esat atvērti?** [vai ɛsat atve:rti?]

When do you open?

Cikos jūs atverieties?
[tsikɔs juːs atveriɛtiɛs?]

When do you close?

Līdz cikiem jūs strādājiet?
[liːdz tsikiɛm juːs straːdaːjiɛt?]

Money

money
nauda
[nauda]

cash
skaidra nauda
[skaidra nauda]

paper money
papīra nauda
[papi:ra nauda]

loose change
sīknauda
[si:knauda]

check | change | tip
čeks | atlikums | dzeramnauda
[re:tʲins | atlikums | dzɛramnauda]

credit card
kredītkarte
[kredi:tkarte]

wallet
maks
[maku]

to buy
pirkt
[pirkt]

to pay
maksāt
[maksa:t]

fine
sods
[sɔds]

free
bez maksas
[bez maksas]

Where can I buy ...?
Kur es varu nopirkt ...?
[kur es varu nɔpirkt ...?]

Is the bank open now?
Vai tagad banka ir atvērta?
[vai tagad banka ir atve:rta?]

When does it open?
No cikiem tā ir atvērta?
[nɔ tsikiɛm ta: ir atve:rta?]

When does it close?
Līdz cikiem tā strādā?
[li:dz tsikiɛm ta: stra:da:?]

How much?
Cik maksā?
[tsik maksa:?]

How much is this?
Cik tas maksā?
[tsik tas maksa:?]

That's too expensive.
Tas ir par dārgu.
[tas ir par da:rgu.]

Excuse me, where do I pay?
Atvainojiet, kur es varu samaksāt?
[atvainɔjiɛt, kur es varu samaksa:t?]

Check, please.
Rēķinu, lūdzu.
[re:tʲinu, lu:dzu.]

Can I pay by credit card?

Is there an ATM here?

I'm looking for an ATM.

Vai varu samaksāt ar karti?
[vai varu samaksa:t ar karti?]
Vai šeit ir bankomāts?
[vai ʃɛit ir bankɔma:ts?]
Es meklēju bankomātu.
[es mekle:ju bankɔma:tu.]

I'm looking for a foreign exchange office.

I'd like to change ...

What is the exchange rate?

Do you need my passport?

Es meklēju valūtas maiņas punktu.
[es mekle:ju valu:tas maiɲas punktu.]
Es vēlos samainīt ...
[es ve:lɔs samaini:t ...]
Kāds ir valūtas kurss?
[ka:ds ir valu:tas kurs?]
Vai jums vajag manu pasi?
[vai jums vajag manu pasi?]

Time

What time is it?	**Cik pulkstens?** [tsik pulkstens?]
When?	**Kad?** [kad?]
At what time?	**Cikos?** [tsikɔs?]
now | later | after …	**tagad | vēlāk | pēc …** [tagad | vɛ:la:k | pe:ts …]

one o'clock	**pulkstens viens** [pulkstens viɛns]
one fifteen	**piecpadsmit pāri vieniem** [piɛtspadsmit pa:ri viɛniɛm]
one thirty	**pusdivi** [pusdivi]
one forty-five	**bez piecpadsmt divi** [bez piɛtspadsmt divi]

one | two | three	**viens | divi | trīs** [viɛns | divi | tri:s]
four | five | six	**četri | pieci | seši** [tʃetri | piɛtsi | seʃi]
seven | eight | nine	**septiņi | astoņi | deviņi** [septiɲi | astɔɲi | deviɲi]
ten | eleven | twelve	**desmit | vienpadsmit | divpadsmit** [desmit | viɛnpadsmit | divpadsmit]

in …	**pēc …** [pe:ts …]
five minutes	**piecām minūtēm** [piɛtsa:m minu:te:m]
ten minutes	**desmit minūtēm** [desmit minu:te:m]
fifteen minutes	**piecpadsmit minūtēm** [piɛtspadsmit minu:te:m]
twenty minutes	**divdesmit minūtēm** [divdesmit minu:te:m]

half an hour	**pusstundas** [pustundas]
an hour	**stundas** [stundas]

in the morning	**no rīta** [nɔ riːta]
early in the morning	**agri no rīta** [agri nɔ riːta]
this morning	**šorīt** [ʃɔriːt]
tomorrow morning	**rīt no rīta** [riːt nɔ riːta]
in the middle of the day	**pusdienlaikā** [pusdiɛnlaika:]
in the afternoon	**pēcpusdienā** [peːtspusdiɛna:]
in the evening	**vakarā** [vakara:]
tonight	**šovakar** [ʃɔvakar]
at night	**naktī** [nakti:]
yesterday	**vakar** [vakar]
today	**šodien** [ʃɔdiɛn]
tomorrow	**rīt** [ri:t]
the day after tomorrow	**parīt** [pari:t]
What day is it today?	**Kas šodien par dienu?** [kas ʃɔdiɛn par diɛnu?]
It's ...	**Šodien ir ...** [ʃɔdiɛn ir ...]
Monday	**Pirmdiena** [pirmdiɛna]
Tuesday	**Otrdiena** [ɔtrdiɛna]
Wednesday	**Trešdiena** [treʃdiɛna]
Thursday	**Ceturtdiena** [tsɛturtdiɛna]
Friday	**Piektdiena** [piɛktdiɛna]
Saturday	**Sestdiena** [sestdiɛna]
Sunday	**Svētdiena** [sveːtdiɛna]

Greetings. Introductions

Hello.
Sveicināti.
[svɛitsina:ti.]

Pleased to meet you.
Priecājos ar jums iepazīties.
[priɛtsa:jɔs ar jums iɛpazi:tiɛs.]

Me too.
Es arī.
[es ari:.]

I'd like you to meet ...
Es vēlos jūs iepazīstināt ar ...
[es ve:lɔs ju:s iɛpazi:stina:t ar ...]

Nice to meet you.
Ļoti patīkami.
[ʎɔti pati:kami.]

How are you?
Kā jums klājas?
[ka: jums kla:jas?]

My name is ...
Mani sauc ...
[mani sauts ...]

His name is ...
Viņu sauc ...
[viɲu sauts ...]

Her name is ...
Viņu sauc ...
[viɲu sauts ...]

What's your name?
Kā jūs sauc?
[ka: ju:s sauts?]

What's his name?
Kā viņu sauc?
[ka: viɲu sauts?]

What's her name?
Kā viņu sauc?
[ka: viɲu sauts?]

What's your last name?
Kāds ir jūsu uzvārds?
[ka:ds ir ju:su uzva:rds?]

You can call me ...
Sauciet mani ...
[sautsiɛt mani ...]

Where are you from?
No kurienes jūs esat?
[nɔ kuriɛnes ju:s ɛsat?]

I'm from ...
Esmu no ...
[ɛsmu nɔ ...]

What do you do for a living?
Kāda ir jūsu nodarbošanās?
[ka:da ir ju:su nɔdarbɔʃana:s?]

Who is this?
Kas tas /tā/ ir?
[kas tas /ta:/ ir?]

Who is he?
Kas viņš ir?
[kas viɲʃ ir?]

Who is she?
Kas viņa ir?
[kas viɲa ir?]

Who are they?	**Kas viņi /viņas/ ir?**
	[kas viņi /viņas/ ir?]
This is …	**Tas /tā/ ir …**
	[tas /ta:/ ir …]
my friend (masc.)	**mans draugs**
	[mans draugs]
my friend (fem.)	**mana draudzene**
	[mana draudzɛne]
my husband	**mans vīrs**
	[mans vi:rs]
my wife	**mana sieva**
	[mana siɛva]
my father	**mans tēvs**
	[mans te:vs]
my mother	**mana māte**
	[mana ma:te]
my brother	**mans brālis**
	[mans bra:lis]
my sister	**mana māsa**
	[mana ma:sa]
my son	**mans dēls**
	[mans dɛ:ls]
my daughter	**mana meita**
	[mana mɛita]
This is our son.	**Šis ir mūsu dēls.**
	[ʃis ir mu:su dɛ:ls.]
This is our daughter.	**Šī ir mūsu meita.**
	[ʃi: ir mu:su mɛita.]
These are my children.	**Šie ir mani bērni.**
	[ʃiɛ ir mani be:rni.]
These are our children.	**Šie ir mūsu bērni.**
	[ʃiɛ ir mu:su be:rni.]

Farewells

Good bye!

Bye! (inform.)

See you tomorrow.

See you soon.

See you at seven.

Uz redzēšanos!
[uz redze:ʃanɔs!]
Atā!
[ata:!]
Līdz rītam.
[li:dz ri:tam.]
Uz tikšanos.
[uz tikʃanɔs.]
Tiekamies septiņos.
[tiɛkamies septiɲɔs.]

Have fun!

Talk to you later.

Have a nice weekend.

Good night.

Izpriecājaties!
[izpriɛtsa:jatiɛs!]
Parunāsim vēlāk.
[paruna:sim vɛ:la:k.]
Lai tev laba nedēļas nogale.
[lai tev laba nɛdɛ:lʲas nɔgale.]
Arlabunakt.
[arlabunakt.]

It's time for me to go.

I have to go.

I will be right back.

Man laiks doties.
[man laiks dɔtiɛs.]
Man jāiet.
[man ja:iɛt.]
Es tūlīt būšu atpakaļ.
[es tu:li:t bu:ʃu atpakalʲ.]

It's late.

I have to get up early.

I'm leaving tomorrow.

We're leaving tomorrow.

Jau vēls.
[jau vɛ:ls.]
Man agri jāceļas.
[man agri ja:tsɛlʲas.]
Es rīt aizbraucu.
[es ri:t aizbrautsu.]
Mēs rīt aizbraucam.
[me:s ri:t aizbrautsam.]

Have a nice trip!

It was nice meeting you.

It was nice talking to you.

Thanks for everything.

Laimīgu ceļojumu!
[laimi:gu tselʲɔjumu!]
Bija prieks ar jums iepazīties.
[bija priɛks ar jums iɛpazi:tiɛs.]
Bija prieks ar jums sarunāties.
[bija priɛks ar jums saruna:tiɛs.]
Paldies par visu.
[paldies par visu.]

I had a very good time. | **Es patīkami pavadīju laiku.**
[es pati:kami pavadi:ju laiku.]

We had a very good time. | **Mēs patīkami pavadījām laiku.**
[me:s pati:kami pavadi:ja:m laiku.]

It was really great. | **Viss bija lieliski.**
[vis bija liɛliski.]

I'm going to miss you. | **Man jūs pietrūks.**
[man ju:s piɛtru:ks.]

We're going to miss you. | **Mums jūs pietrūks.**
[mums ju:s piɛtru:ks.]

Good luck! | **Lai veicas!**
[lai vɛitsas!]

Say hi to ... | **Pasveiciniet ...**
[pasvɛitsiniɛt ...]

Foreign language

I don't understand.	**Es nesaprotu.** [es nɛsaprɔtu.]
Write it down, please.	**Lūdzu, uzrakstiet to.** [lu:dzu, uzrakstiɛt tɔ.]
Do you speak ...?	**Vai jūs runājat ...?** [vai ju:s runa:jat ...?]

I speak a little bit of ...	**Es nedaudz protu ...** [es nɛdaudz prɔtu ...]
English	**angļu valodu** [aŋglʲu valɔdu]
Turkish	**turku valodu** [turku valɔdu]
Arabic	**arābu valodu** [ara:bu valɔdu]
French	**franču valodu** [frantʃu valɔdu]

German	**vācu valodu** [va:tsu valɔdu]
Italian	**itāļu valodu** [ita:lʲu valɔdu]
Spanish	**spāņu valodu** [spa:ɲu valɔdu]
Portuguese	**portugāļu valodu** [pɔrtuga:lʲu valɔdu]
Chinese	**ķīniešu valodu** [tʲi:niɛʃu valɔdu]
Japanese	**japāņu valodu** [japa:ɲu valɔdu]

Can you repeat that, please.	**Lūdzu, atkārtojiet.** [lu:dzu, atka:rtɔjiɛt.]
I understand.	**Es saprotu.** [es saprɔtu.]
I don't understand.	**Es nesaprotu.** [es nɛsaprɔtu.]
Please speak more slowly.	**Lūdzu, runājiet lēnāk.** [lu:dzu, runa:jiɛt lɛ:na:k.]

Is that correct? (Am I saying it right?)	**Vai pareizi?** [vai parɛizi?]
What is this? (What does this mean?)	**Kas tas ir?** [kas tas ir?]

Apologies

Excuse me, please.

Atvainojiet, lūdzu.
[atvainɔjiɛt, luːdzu.]

I'm sorry.

Man žēl.
[man ʒeːl.]

I'm really sorry.

Man ļoti žēl.
[man ʎɔti ʒeːl.]

Sorry, it's my fault.

Atvainojiet, tā ir mana vaina.
[atvainɔjiɛt, taː ir mana vaina.]

My mistake.

Mana kļūda.
[mana kʎuːda.]

May I ...?

Vai drīkstu ...?
[vai driːkstu ...?]

Do you mind if I ...?

Vai jums nav nekas pretī, ja es ...?
[vai jums nav nɛkas pretiː, ja es ...?]

It's OK.

Tas nekas.
[tas nɛkas.]

It's all right.

Viss kārtībā.
[vis kaːrtiːbaː.]

Don't worry about it.

Neuztraucieties.
[nɛuztrautsiɛtiɛs.]

Agreement

Yes.	**Jā.** [ja:.]
Yes, sure.	**Jā, protams.** [ja:, prɔtams.]
OK (Good!)	**Labi!** [labi!]
Very well.	**Ļoti labi.** [ḷɔti labi.]
Certainly!	**Protams!** [prɔtams!]
I agree.	**Es piekrītu.** [es piɛkri:tu.]
That's correct.	**Taisnība.** [taisni:ba.]
That's right.	**Pareizi.** [parɛizi.]
You're right.	**Jums taisnība.** [jums taisni:ba.]
I don't mind.	**Man nav iebildumu.** [man nav iɛbildumu.]
Absolutely right.	**Pilnīgi pareizi.** [pilni:gi parɛizi.]
It's possible.	**Tas ir iespējams.** [tas ir iɛspe:jams.]
That's a good idea.	**Tā ir laba doma.** [ta: ir laba dɔma.]
I can't say no.	**Es nevaru atteikt.** [es nɛvaru attɛikt.]
I'd be happy to.	**Priecāšos.** [priɛtsa:ʃɔs.]
With pleasure.	**Ar prieku.** [ar priɛku.]

Refusal. Expressing doubt

No.	**Nē.** [ne:.]
Certainly not.	**Noteikti, nē.** [nɔtɛikti, ne:.]
I don't agree.	**Es nepiekrītu.** [es nepiɛkri:tu.]
I don't think so.	**Es tā nedomāju.** [es ta: nedɔma:ju.]
It's not true.	**Tā nav taisnība.** [ta: nav taisni:ba.]
You are wrong.	**Jums nav taisnība.** [jums nav taisni:ba.]
I think you are wrong.	**Es domāju, jums nav taisnība.** [es dɔma:ju, jums nav taisni:ba.]
I'm not sure.	**Neesmu drošs.** [neesmu drɔʃs.]
It's impossible.	**Tas nav iespējams.** [tas nav iɛspe:jams.]
Nothing of the kind (sort)!	**Nekas tamlīdzīgs.** [nɛkas tamli:dzi:gs.]
The exact opposite.	**Tieši pretēji.** [tiɛʃi prɛte:ji.]
I'm against it.	**Esmu pret.** [ɛsmu pret.]
I don't care.	**Man vienalga.** [man viɛnalga.]
I have no idea.	**Man nav ne jausmas.** [man nav ne jausmas.]
I doubt it.	**Šaubos, ka tas tā ir.** [ʃaubɔs, ka tas ta: ir.]
Sorry, I can't.	**Atvainojiet, es nevaru.** [atvainɔjiɛt, es nɛvaru.]
Sorry, I don't want to.	**Atvainojiet, es negribu.** [atvainɔjiɛt, es negribu.]
Thank you, but I don't need this.	**Paldies, bet man tas nav vajadzīgs.** [paldiɛs, bet man tas nav vajadzi:gs.]
It's getting late.	**Jau vēls.** [jau vɛ:ls.]

I have to get up early.

Man agri jāceļas.
[man agri jaːtsɛlʲas.]

I don't feel well.

Man ir slikti.
[man ir slikti.]

Expressing gratitude

Thank you.	**Paldies.** [paldiɛs.]
Thank you very much.	**Liels paldies.** [liɛls paldiɛs.]
I really appreciate it.	**Esmu ļoti pateicīgs /pateicīga/.** [ɛsmu ļoti patɛitsi:gs /patɛitsi:ga/.]
I'm really grateful to you.	**Es pateicos jums.** [es patɛitsɔs jums.]
We are really grateful to you.	**Mēs pateicamies jums.** [me:s patɛitsamies jums.]

Thank you for your time.	**Paldies, ka veltījāt laiku.** [paldiɛs, ka velti:ja:t laiku.]
Thanks for everything.	**Paldies par visu.** [paldies par visu.]
Thank you for ...	**Paldies par ...** [paldies par ...]
your help	**palīdzību** [pali:dzi:bu]
a nice time	**labi pavadītu laiku** [labi pavadi:tu laiku]

a wonderful meal	**brīnišķīgu maltīti** [bri:niʃḱi:gu malti:ti]
a pleasant evening	**patīkamu vakaru** [pati:kamu vakaru]
a wonderful day	**lielisku dienu** [liɛlisku diɛnu]
an amazing journey	**pārsteidzošo braucienu** [pa:rstɛidzɔʃo brautsiɛnu]

Don't mention it.	**Nav par ko.** [nav par kɔ.]
You are welcome.	**Nav vērts pieminēt.** [nav ve:rts piɛmine:t.]
Any time.	**Jebkurā laikā.** [jebkura: laika:.]
My pleasure.	**Bija prieks palīdzēt.** [bija priɛks pali:dze:t.]
Forget it.	**Aizmirstiet. Viss kārtībā.** [aizmirstiɛt. vis ka:rti:ba:.]
Don't worry about it.	**Neuztraucieties.** [nɛuztrautsiɛtiɛs.]

Congratulations. Best wishes

Congratulations!
Apsveicu!
[apsvɛitsu!]

Happy birthday!
Daudz laimes dzimšanas dienā!
[daudz laimes dzimʃanas diɛna:!]

Merry Christmas!
Priecīgus Ziemassvētkus!
[priɛtsi:gus ziɛmasve:tkus!]

Happy New Year!
Laimīgu Jauno gadu!
[laimi:gu jaunɔ gadu!]

Happy Easter!
Priecīgas Lieldienas!
[priɛtsi:gas liɛldiɛnas!]

Happy Hanukkah!
Priecīgu Hanuku!
[priɛtsi:gu xanuku!]

I'd like to propose a toast.
Es vēlos teikt tostu.
[es ve:lɔs tɛikt tɔstu.]

Cheers!
Priekā!
[priɛka:!]

Let's drink to …!
Uz … veselību!
[uz … vɛseli:bu!]

To our success!
Par mūsu panākumiem!
[par mu:su pana:kumiɛm!]

To your success!
Par jūsu panākumiem!
[par ju:su pana:kumiɛm!]

Good luck!
Lai veicas!
[lai vɛitsas!]

Have a nice day!
Lai jums jauka diena!
[lai jums jauka diɛna!]

Have a good holiday!
Lai jums labas brīvdienas!
[lai jums labas bri:vdiɛnas!]

Have a safe journey!
Lai jums veiksmīgs ceļojums!
[lai jums vɛiksmi:gs tseļʲojums!]

I hope you get better soon!
Novēlu jums ātru atveseļošanos!
[nɔve:lu jums a:tru atvɛseļʲɔʃanɔs!]

Socializing

Why are you sad?	**Kāpēc jūs esat noskumis /noskumusi/?** [ka:pe:ts ju:s ɛsat nɔskumis /nɔskumusi/?]
Smile! Cheer up!	**Pasmaidiet!** [pasmaidiɛt!]
Are you free tonight?	**Vai esat aizņemts /aizņemta/ šovakar?** [vai ɛsat aizɲemts /aizɲemta/ ʃovakar?]
May I offer you a drink?	**Vai drīkstu jums uzsaukt dzērienu?** [vai dri:kstu jums uzsaukt dze:riɛnu?]
Would you like to dance?	**Vai vēlaties padejot?** [vai vɛ:laties padejɔt?]
Let's go to the movies.	**Varbūt aizejam uz kino?** [varbu:t aizejam uz kinɔ?]
May I invite you to ...?	**Vai drīkstu jūs aicināt uz ...?** [vai dri:kstu ju:s aitsina:t uz ...?]
a restaurant	**restorānu** [restɔra:nu]
the movies	**kino** [kinɔ]
the theater	**teātri** [tea:tri]
go for a walk	**pastaigu** [pastaigu]
At what time?	**Cikos?** [tsikɔs?]
tonight	**šovakar** [ʃovakar]
at six	**sešos** [seʃɔs]
at seven	**septiņos** [septiɲɔs]
at eight	**astošos** [astɔʃɔs]
at nine	**deviņos** [deviɲɔs]
Do you like it here?	**Vai jums te patīk?** [vai jums te pati:k?]
Are you here with someone?	**Vai jūs esat šeit ar kādu?** [vai ju:s ɛsat ʃɛit ar ka:du?]

I'm with my friend.

Esmu ar draugu /draudzeni/.
[ɛsmu ar draugu /draudzeni/.]

I'm with my friends.

Esmu ar saviem draugiem.
[ɛsmu ar saviɛm draugiɛm.]

No, I'm alone.

Nē, esmu viens /viena/.
[ne:, esmu viɛns /viɛna/.]

Do you have a boyfriend?

Vai jums ir puisis?
[vai jums ir puisis?]

I have a boyfriend.

Man ir puisis.
[man ir puisis.]

Do you have a girlfriend?

Vai jums ir meitene?
[vai jums ir mɛitɛne?]

I have a girlfriend.

Man ir meitene,
[man ir mɛitɛne,]

Can I see you again?

Vai mēs vēl tiksimies?
[vai me:s ve:l tiksimiɛs?]

Can I call you?

Vai drīkstu tev piezvanīt?
[vai dri:kstu tev piɛzvani:t?]

Call me. (Give me a call.)

Piezvani man.
[piɛzvani man.]

What's your number?

Kāds ir tavs numurs?
[ka:ds ir tavs numurs?]

I miss you.

Man tevis pietrūkst.
[man tevis piɛtru:kst.]

You have a beautiful name.

Jums ir skaists vārds.
[jums ir skaists va:rds.]

I love you.

Es tevi mīlu.
[es tevi mi:lu.]

Will you marry me?

Vai precēsi mani.
[vai pretse:si mani.]

You're kidding!

Jūs jokojat?
[ju:s jɔkɔjat?]

I'm just kidding.

Es tikai jokoju.
[es tikai jɔkɔju.]

Are you serious?

Vai jūs nopietni?
[vai ju:s nɔpiɛtni?]

I'm serious.

Es runāju nopietni.
[es runa:ju nɔpiɛtni.]

Really?!

Tiešām?!
[tiɛʃa:m?!]

It's unbelievable!

Tas ir neticami!
[tas ir netitsami!]

I don't believe you.

Es jums neticu!
[es jums netitsu!]

I can't.

Es nevaru.
[es nɛvaru.]

I don't know.

Es nezinu.
[es nezinu.]

I don't understand you.　　**Es jūs nesaprotu.**
[es ju:s nɛsaprotu.]

Please go away.　　**Lūdzu, ejiet prom.**
[lu:dzu, ejiɛt prɔm.]

Leave me alone!　　**Atstājiet mani vienu!**
[atsta:jiɛt mani viɛnu!]

I can't stand him.　　**Es nevaru viņu ciest.**
[es nɛvaru viɲu tsiɛst.]

You are disgusting!　　**Jūs esat pretīgs!**
[ju:s ɛsat preti:gs!]

I'll call the police!　　**Es izsaukšu policīju!**
[es izsaukʃu pɔlitsi:ju!]

Sharing impressions. Emotions

I like it.	**Man patīk.** [man pati:k.]
Very nice.	**Ļoti jauki.** [ʎoti jauki.]
That's great!	**Tas ir lieliski!** [tas ir liɛliski!]
It's not bad.	**Tas nav slikti.** [tas nav slikti.]

I don't like it.	**Man nepatīk.** [man nɛpati:k.]
It's not good.	**Tas nav labi.** [tas nav labi.]
It's bad.	**Tas ir slikti.** [tas ir slikti.]
It's very bad.	**Tas ir ļoti slikti.** [tas ir ʎoti slikti.]
It's disgusting.	**Tas ir pretīgi.** [tas ir preti:gi.]

I'm happy.	**Esmu laimīgs /laimīga/.** [ɛsmu laimi:gs /laimi:ga/.]
I'm content.	**Esmu apmierināts /apmierināta/.** [ɛsmu apmiɛrina:ts /apmiɛrina:ta/.]
I'm in love.	**Esmu iemīlējies /iemīlējusies/.** [ɛsmu iɛmi:le:jies /iɛmi:le:jusiɛs/.]
I'm calm.	**Esmu mierīgs /mierīga/.** [ɛsmu miɛri:gs /miɛri:ga/.]
I'm bored.	**Man ir garlaicīgi.** [man ir garlaitsi:gi.]

I'm tired.	**Es esmu noguris /nogurusi/.** [es esmu nɔguris /nɔgurusi/.]
I'm sad.	**Man ir skumji.** [man ir skumji.]
I'm frightened.	**Man ir bail.** [man ir bail.]
I'm angry.	**Esmu dusmīgs /dusmīga/.** [ɛsmu dusmi:gs /dusmi:ga/.]

I'm worried.	**Esmu uztraucies /uztraukusies/.** [ɛsmu uztrautsies /uztraukusiɛs/.]
I'm nervous.	**Esmu nervozs /nervoza/.** [ɛsmu nervɔzs /nervɔza/.]

I'm jealous. (envious)	**Es apskaužu.** [es apskauʒu.]
I'm surprised.	**Esmu pārsteigts /pārsteigta/.** [ɛsmu paːrstɛigts /paːrstɛigta/.]
I'm perplexed.	**Esmu apjucis /apjukusi/.** [ɛsmu apjutsis /apjukusi/.]

Problems. Accidents

I've got a problem.	**Man ir problēma.** [man ir problɛ:ma.]
We've got a problem.	**Mums ir problēma.** [mums ir problɛ:ma.]
I'm lost.	**Esmu apmaldījies /apmaldījusies/.** [ɛsmu apmaldi:jies /apmaldi:jusiɛs/.]
I missed the last bus (train).	**Es nokavēju pēdējo autobusu (vilcienu).** [es nɔkave:ju pɛ:de:jɔ autɔbusu.]
I don't have any money left.	**Man vairs nav naudas.** [man vairs nav naudas.]

I've lost my ...	**Es pazaudēju savu ...** [es pazaude:ju savu ...]
Someone stole my ...	**Kāds nozaga manu ...** [ka:ds nɔzaga manu ...]

passport	**pasi** [pasi]
wallet	**maku** [maku]
papers	**dokumentus** [dɔkumentus]
ticket	**biļeti** [biḷeti]

money	**naudu** [naudu]
handbag	**rokassomiņu** [rɔkasɔmiɲu]
camera	**fotoaparātu** [fɔtɔapara:tu]
laptop	**klēpjdatoru** [kle:pjdatɔru]
tablet computer	**planšetdatoru** [planʃetdatɔru]
mobile phone	**mobīlo telefonu** [mɔbi:lɔ tɛlefɔnu]

Help me!	**Palīgā!** [pali:ga:!]
What's happened?	**Kas noticis?** [kas nɔtitsis?]

fire	**ugunsgrēks** [ugunsgre:ks]
shooting	**apšaude** [ʃauʃana]
murder	**slepkavība** [slepkavi:ba]
explosion	**sprādziens** [spra:dziɛns]
fight	**kautiņš** [kautiɲʃ]

Call the police!	**Izauciet policiju!** [izautsiɛt pɔlitsi:ju!]
Please hurry up!	**Lūdzu, pasteidzieties!** [lu:dzu, pastɛidziɛtiɛs!]
I'm looking for the police station.	**Es meklēju policijas iecirkni.** [es mekle:ju pɔlitsi:jas iɛtsirkni.]
I need to make a call.	**Man jāpezvana.** [man ja:pezvana.]
May I use your phone?	**Vai drīkstu piezvanīt?** [vai dri:kstu piɛzvani:t?]

I've been ...	**Mani ...** [mani ...]
mugged	**aplaupīja** [aplaupi:ja]
robbed	**apzaga** [apzaga]
raped	**izvaroja** [izvarɔja]
attacked (beaten up)	**piekāva** [piɛka:va]

Are you all right?	**Vai jums viss kārtībā?** [vai jums vis ka:rti:ba:?]
Did you see who it was?	**Vai jūs redzējāt, kurš tas bija?** [vai ju:s redze:ja:t, kurʃ tas bija?]
Would you be able to recognize the person?	**Vai jūs varēsiet viņu atpazīt?** [vai ju:s vare:siɛt viɲu atpazi:t?]
Are you sure?	**Vai esat drošs /droša/?** [vai ɛsat drɔʃs /drɔʃa/?]

Please calm down.	**Lūdzu, nomierinieties.** [lu:dzu, nɔmiɛriniɛtiɛs.]
Take it easy!	**Mierīgāk!** [miɛri:ga:k!]
Don't worry!	**Neuztraucieties!** [nɛuztrautsiɛtiɛs!]
Everything will be fine.	**Viss būs labi.** [vis bu:s labi.]
Everything's all right.	**Viss kārtībā.** [vis ka:rti:ba:.]

Come here, please.

Nāciet šurp, lūdzu.
[na:tsiɛt ʃurp, lu:dzu.]

I have some questions for you.

Man jāuzdod jums daži jautājumi.
[man ja:uzdod jums daʒi jauta:jumi.]

Wait a moment, please.

Uzgaidiet, lūdzu.
[uzgaidiɛt, lu:dzu.]

Do you have any I.D.?

Vai jums ir dokumenti?
[vai jums ir dɔkumenti?]

Thanks. You can leave now.

Paldies. Jūs variet iet.
[paldiɛs. ju:s variɛt iɛt.]

Hands behind your head!

Rokas aiz galvas!
[rɔkas aiz galvas!]

You're under arrest!

Jūs esat arestēts /arestēta/!
[ju:s ɛsat areste:ts /arestɛ:ta/!]

Health problems

Please help me.	**Lūdzu, palīdziet.** [luːdzu, paliːdziɛt.]
I don't feel well.	**Man ir slikti.** [man ir slikti.]
My husband doesn't feel well.	**Manam vīram ir slikti.** [manam viːram ir slikti.]
My son …	**Manam dēlam …** [manam dɛːlam …]
My father …	**Manam tēvam …** [manam tɛːvam …]

My wife doesn't feel well.	**Manai sievai ir slikti.** [manai siɛvai ir slikti.]
My daughter …	**Manai meitai …** [manai mɛitai …]
My mother …	**Manai mātei …** [manai maːtɛi …]

I've got a …	**Man sāp …** [man saːp …]
headache	**galva** [galva]
sore throat	**kakls** [kakls]
stomach ache	**vēders** [vɛːdɛrs]
toothache	**zobs** [zɔbs]

I feel dizzy.	**Man reibst galva.** [man rɛibst galva.]
He has a fever.	**Viņam ir drudzis.** [viɲam ir drudzis.]
She has a fever.	**Viņai ir drudzis.** [viɲai ir drudzis.]
I can't breathe.	**Es nevaru paelpot.** [es nɛvaru paelpɔt.]

I'm short of breath.	**Man trūkst elpas.** [man truːkst elpas.]
I am asthmatic.	**Man ir astma.** [man ir astma.]
I am diabetic.	**Man ir diabēts.** [man ir diabeːts.]

| I can't sleep. | **Man ir bezmiegs.**
[man ir bezmiɛgs.] |
| food poisoning | **saindēšanās ar ēdienu**
[sainde:ʃana:s ar e:diɛnu] |

It hurts here.	**Man sāp šeit.** [man sa:p ʃɛit.]
Help me!	**Palīgā!** [pali:ga:!]
I am here!	**Es esmu šeit!** [es esmu ʃɛit!]
We are here!	**Mēs esam šeit!** [me:s ɛsam ʃɛit!]
Get me out of here!	**Daboniet mani arā no šejienes!** [dabɔniɛt mani ara: nɔ ʃejiɛnes!]
I need a doctor.	**Man vajag ārstu.** [man vajag a:rstu.]
I can't move.	**Es nevaru pakustēties.** [es nɛvaru pakuste:tiɛs.]
I can't move my legs.	**Es nevaru pakustināt kājas.** [es nɛvaru pakustina:t ka:jas.]

I have a wound.	**Es esmu ievainots /ievainota/.** [es esmu iɛvainɔts /iɛvainɔta/.]
Is it serious?	**Vai kas nopietns?** [vai kas nɔpiɛtns?]
My documents are in my pocket.	**Mani dokumenti ir kabatā.** [mani dɔkumenti ir kabata:.]
Calm down!	**Nomierinieties!** [nɔmiɛriniɛtiɛs!]
May I use your phone?	**Vai drīkstu piezvanīt?** [vai dri:kstu piɛzvani:t?]

Call an ambulance!	**Izsauciet ātro palīdzību!** [izsautsiɛt a:trɔ pali:dzi:bu!]
It's urgent!	**Tas ir steidzami!** [tas ir stɛidzami!]
It's an emergency!	**Tas ir ļoti steidzami!** [tas ir ļoti stɛidzami!]
Please hurry up!	**Lūdzu, pasteidzieties!** [lu:dzu, pastɛidziɛtiɛs!]
Would you please call a doctor?	**Lūdzu, izsauciet ārstu!** [lu:dzu, izsautsiɛt a:rstu!]
Where is the hospital?	**Kur ir slimnīca?** [kur ir slimni:tsa?]

How are you feeling?	**Kā jūs jūtaties** [ka: ju:s ju:tatiɛs]
Are you all right?	**Vai jums viss kārtībā?** [vai jums vis ka:rti:ba:?]
What's happened?	**Kas noticis?** [kas nɔtitsis?]

I feel better now. **Es jūtos labāk.**
[es ju:tɔs laba:k.]

It's OK. **Viss kārtībā.**
[vis ka:rti:ba:.]

It's all right. **Viss ir labi.**
[vis ir labi.]

At the pharmacy

pharmacy (drugstore)	**aptieka** [aptiɛka]
24-hour pharmacy	**diennakts aptieka** [diɛnnakts aptiɛka]
Where is the closest pharmacy?	**Kur ir tuvākā aptieka?** [kur ir tuva:ka: aptiɛka?]
Is it open now?	**Vai tagad tā ir atvērta.** [vai tagad ta: ir atve:rta.]
At what time does it open?	**Cikos tā būs atvērta?** [tsikɔs ta: bu:s atve:rta?]
At what time does it close?	**Līdz cikiem tā strādā?** [li:dz tsikiɛm ta: stra:da:?]
Is it far?	**Vai tas ir tālu?** [vai tas ir ta:lu?]
Can I get there on foot?	**Vai es aiziešu ar kājām?** [vai es aiziɛʃu ar ka:ja:m?]
Can you show me on the map?	**Lūdzu, parādiet to uz kartes?** [lu:dzu, para:diɛt tɔ uz kartes?]
Please give me something for …	**Lūdzu, dodiet man kaut ko pret …** [lu:dzu, dɔdiɛt man kaut kɔ pret …]
a headache	**galvassāpēm** [galvasa:pe:m]
a cough	**klepu** [klɛpu]
a cold	**saaukstēšanos** [saaukste:ʃanɔs]
the flu	**gripu** [gripu]
a fever	**drudzi** [drudzi]
a stomach ache	**vēdersāpēm** [vɛ:dɛrsa:pe:m]
nausea	**sliktu dūšu** [sliktu du:ʃu]
diarrhea	**caureju** [tsaureju]
constipation	**aizcietējumu** [aiztsiɛtɛ:jumu]
pain in the back	**muguras sāpēm** [muguras sa:pe:m]

chest pain	sāpēm krūtīs [sa:pe:m kru:ti:s]
side stitch	sāpēm sānos [sa:pe:m sa:nɔs]
abdominal pain	vēdera sāpēm [vɛ:dɛra sa:pe:m]

pill	tablete [tablɛte]
ointment, cream	ziede, krēms [ziɛde, kre:ms]
syrup	sīrups [si:rups]
spray	aerosols [aerɔsɔls]
drops	pilieni [piliɛni]

You need to go to the hospital.	Jums jābrauc uz slimnīcu. [jums ja:brauts uz slimni:tsu.]
health insurance	veselības apdrošināšana [vɛseli:bas apdrɔʃina:ʃana]
prescription	recepte [retsepte]
insect repellant	kukaiņu atbaidīšanas līdzeklis [kukaiņu atbaidi:ʃanas li:dzeklis]
Band Aid	plāksteris [pla:ksteris]

The bare minimum

Excuse me, ...	**Atvainojiet, ...** [atvainɔjiɛt, ...]
Hello.	**Sveicināti.** [svɛitsina:ti.]
Thank you.	**Paldies.** [paldiɛs.]
Good bye.	**Uz redzēšanos.** [uz redze:ʃanɔs.]
Yes.	**Jā.** [ja:.]
No.	**Nē.** [ne:.]
I don't know.	**Es nezinu.** [es nezinu.]
Where? | Where to? | When?	**Kur? | Uz kurieni? | Kad?** [kur? | uz kuriɛni? | kad?]

I need ...	**Man vajag ...** [man vajag ...]
I want ...	**Es gribu ...** [es gribu ...]
Do you have ...?	**Vai jums ir ...?** [vai jums ir ...?]
Is there a ... here?	**Vai šeit ir ...?** [vai ʃɛit ir ...?]
May I ...?	**Vai drīkstu ...?** [vai dri:kstu ...?]
..., please (polite request)	**Lūdzu, ...** [lu:dzu, ...]

I'm looking for ...	**Es meklēju ...** [es mekle:ju ...]
restroom	**tualeti** [tualeti]
ATM	**bankomātu** [bankɔma:tu]
pharmacy (drugstore)	**aptieku** [aptiɛku]
hospital	**slimnīcu** [slimni:tsu]
police station	**policijas iecirkni** [pɔlitsi:jas iɛtsirkni]
subway	**metro** [metrɔ]

taxi	**taksometru** [taksɔmetru]
train station	**dzelzceļa staciju** [dzelztsɛlʲa statsiju]

My name is ...	**Mani sauc ...** [mani sauts ...]
What's your name?	**Kā jūs sauc?** [ka: ju:s sauts?]
Could you please help me?	**Lūdzu, palīdziet.** [lu:dzu, pali:dziɛt.]
I've got a problem.	**Man ir problēma.** [man ir prɔblɛ:ma.]
I don't feel well.	**Man ir slikti.** [man ir slikti.]
Call an ambulance!	**Izsauciet ātro palīdzību!** [izsautsiɛt a:trɔ pali:dzi:bu!]
May I make a call?	**Vai drīkstu piezvanīt?** [vai dri:kstu piɛzvani:t?]

I'm sorry.	**Atvainojos.** [atvainɔjɔs.]
You're welcome.	**Lūdzu.** [lu:dzu.]

I, me	**es** [es]
you (inform.)	**tu** [tu]
he	**viņš** [viɲʃ]
she	**viņa** [viɲa]
they (masc.)	**viņi** [viɲi]
they (fem.)	**viņas** [viɲas]
we	**mēs** [me:s]
you (pl)	**jūs** [ju:s]
you (sg, form.)	**Jūs** [ju:s]

ENTRANCE	**IEEJA** [iɛeja]
EXIT	**IZEJA** [izeja]
OUT OF ORDER	**NESTRĀDĀ** [nestra:da:]
CLOSED	**SLĒGTS** [sle:gts]

OPEN	**ATVĒRTS** [atve:rts]
FOR WOMEN	**SIEVIETĒM** [siɛviɛte:m]
FOR MEN	**VĪRIEŠIEM** [vi:riɛʃiɛm]

MINI DICTIONARY

This section contains 250 useful words required for everyday communication. You will find the names of months and days of the week here. The dictionary also contains topics such as colors, measurements, family, and more

T&P Books Publishing

DICTIONARY CONTENTS

T&P Books Publishing

time	**laiks** (v)	[laiks]
hour	**stunda** (s)	[stunda]
half an hour	**pusstunda**	[pustunda]
minute	**minūte** (s)	[minu:te]
second	**sekunde** (s)	[sɛkunde]
today (adv)	**šodien**	[ʃɔdiɛn]
tomorrow (adv)	**rīt**	[ri:t]
yesterday (adv)	**vakar**	[vakar]
Monday	**pirmdiena** (s)	[pirmdiɛna]
Tuesday	**otrdiena** (s)	[ɔtrdiɛna]
Wednesday	**trešdiena** (s)	[treʃdiɛna]
Thursday	**ceturtdiena** (s)	[tsɛturtdiɛna]
Friday	**piektdiena** (s)	[piɛktdiɛna]
Saturday	**sestdiena** (s)	[sestdiɛna]
Sunday	**svētdiena** (s)	[sve:tdiɛna]
day	**diena** (s)	[diɛna]
working day	**darba diena** (s)	[darba diɛna]
public holiday	**svētku diena** (s)	[sve:tku diɛna]
weekend	**brīvdienas** (s dsk)	[bri:vdiɛnas]
week	**nedēļa** (s)	[nɛdɛ:lʲa]
last week (adv)	**pagājušajā nedēļā**	[pɑga:juʃaja nɛdɛ:lʲa:]
next week (adv)	**nākamajā nedēļā**	[na:kamaja: nɛdɛ:lʲa:]
in the morning	**no rīta**	[nɔ ri:ta]
in the afternoon	**pēcpusdienā**	[pe:tspusdiɛna:]
in the evening	**vakarā**	[vakara:]
tonight (this evening)	**šovakar**	[ʃovakar]
at night	**naktī**	[nakti:]
midnight	**pusnakts** (s)	[pusnakts]
January	**janvāris** (v)	[janva:ris]
February	**februāris** (v)	[februa:ris]
March	**marts** (v)	[marts]
April	**aprīlis** (v)	[apri:lis]
May	**maijs** (v)	[maijs]
June	**jūnijs** (v)	[ju:nijs]
July	**jūlijs** (v)	[ju:lijs]
August	**augusts** (v)	[augusts]

September	septembris (v)	[septembris]
October	oktobris (v)	[ɔktɔbris]
November	novembris (v)	[nɔvembris]
December	decembris (v)	[detsembris]

in spring	pavasarī	[pavasari:]
in summer	vasarā	[vasara:]
in fall	rudenī	[rudeni:]
in winter	ziemā	[ziɛma:]

month	mēnesis (v)	[mɛ:nesis]
season (summer, etc.)	gadalaiks (v)	[gadalaiks]
year	gads (v)	[gads]

2. Numbers. Numerals

0 zero	nulle	[nulle]
1 one	viens	[viɛns]
2 two	divi	[divi]
3 three	trīs	[tri:s]
4 four	četri	[tʃetri]

5 five	pieci	[piɛtsi]
6 six	seši	[seʃi]
7 seven	septiņi	[septiɲi]
8 eight	astoņi	[astɔɲi]
9 nine	deviņi	[deviɲi]
10 ten	desmit	[desmit]

11 eleven	vienpadsmit	[viɛnpadsmit]
12 twelve	divpadsmit	[divpadsmit]
13 thirteen	trīspadsmit	[tri:spadsmit]
14 fourteen	četrpadsmit	[tʃetrpadsmit]
15 fifteen	piecpadsmit	[piɛtspadsmit]

16 sixteen	sešpadsmit	[seʃpadsmit]
17 seventeen	septiņpadsmit	[septiɲpadsmit]
18 eighteen	astoņpadsmit	[astɔɲpadsmit]
19 nineteen	deviņpadsmit	[deviɲpadsmit]

20 twenty	divdesmit	[divdesmit]
30 thirty	trīsdesmit	[tri:sdesmit]
40 forty	četrdesmit	[tʃetrdesmit]
50 fifty	piecdesmit	[piɛtsdesmit]

60 sixty	sešdesmit	[seʃdesmit]
70 seventy	septiņdesmit	[septiɲdesmit]
80 eighty	astoņdesmit	[astɔɲdesmit]
90 ninety	deviņdesmit	[deviɲdesmit]
100 one hundred	simts	[simts]

200 two hundred	**divsimt**	[divsimt]
300 three hundred	**trīssimt**	[tri:simt]
400 four hundred	**četrsimt**	[tʃetrsimt]
500 five hundred	**piecsimt**	[piɛtsimt]
600 six hundred	**sešsimt**	[seʃsimt]
700 seven hundred	**septiņsimt**	[septiɲsimt]
800 eight hundred	**astoņsimt**	[astoɲsimt]
900 nine hundred	**deviņsimt**	[deviɲsimt]
1000 one thousand	**tūkstotis**	[tu:kstɔtis]
10000 ten thousand	**desmit tūkstoši**	[desmit tu:kstɔʃi]
one hundred thousand	**simt tūkstoši**	[simt tu:kstɔʃi]
million	**miljons** (v)	[miljɔns]
billion	**miljards** (v)	[miljards]

3. Humans. Family

man (adult male)	**vīrietis** (v)	[vi:riɛtis]
young man	**jauneklis** (v)	[jauneklis]
woman	**sieviete** (s)	[siɛviɛte]
girl (young woman)	**jauniete** (s)	[jauniɛte]
old man	**vecītis** (v)	[vetsi:tis]
old woman	**vecenīte** (s)	[vetseni:te]
mother	**māte** (s)	[ma:te]
father	**tēvs** (v)	[te:vs]
son	**dēls** (v)	[dɛ:ls]
daughter	**meita** (s)	[mɛita]
brother	**brālis** (v)	[bra:lis]
sister	**māsa** (s)	[ma:sa]
parents	**vecāki** (v dsk)	[vetsa:ki]
child	**bērns** (v)	[be:rns]
children	**bērni** (v dsk)	[be:rni]
stepmother	**pamāte** (s)	[pama:te]
stepfather	**patēvs** (v)	[pate:vs]
grandmother	**vecmāmiņa** (s)	[vetsma:miɲa]
grandfather	**vectēvs** (v)	[vetste:vs]
grandson	**mazdēls** (v)	[mazdɛ:ls]
granddaughter	**mazmeita** (s)	[mazmɛita]
grandchildren	**mazbērni** (v dsk)	[mazbe:rni]
uncle	**onkulis** (v)	[ɔnkulis]
aunt	**tante** (s)	[tante]
nephew	**brāļadēls, māsasdēls** (v)	[bra:ɬadɛ:ls], [ma:sasdɛ:ls]
niece	**brāļameita, māsasmeita** (s)	[bra:ɬamɛita], [ma:sasmɛita]

wife	sieva (s)	[siɛva]
husband	vīrs (v)	[vi:rs]
married (masc.)	precējies	[pretse:jiɛs]
married (fem.)	precējusies	[pretse:jusiɛs]
widow	atraitne (s)	[atraitne]
widower	atraitnis (v)	[atraitnis]

| name (first name) | vārds (v) | [va:rds] |
| surname (last name) | uzvārds (v) | [uzva:rds] |

relative	radinieks (v)	[radiniɛks]
friend (masc.)	draugs (v)	[draugs]
friendship	draudzība (s)	[draudzi:ba]

partner	partneris (v)	[partneris]
superior (n)	priekšnieks (v)	[priɛkʃniɛks]
colleague	kolēģis (v)	[kɔle:dʲis]
neighbors	kaimiņi (v dsk)	[kaimiɲi]

4. Human body

body	ķermenis (v)	[tʲermenis]
heart	sirds (s)	[sirds]
blood	asins (s)	[asins]
brain	smadzenes (s dsk)	[smadzɛnes]

bone	kauls (v)	[kauls]
spine (backbone)	mugurkauls (v)	[mugurkauls]
rib	riba (s)	[riba]
lungs	plaušas (s dsk)	[plauʃas]
skin	āda (s)	[a:da]

head	galva (s)	[galva]
face	seja (s)	[seja]
nose	deguns (v)	[dɛguns]
forehead	piere (s)	[piɛre]
cheek	vaigs (v)	[vaigs]

mouth	mute (s)	[mute]
tongue	mēle (s)	[mɛ:le]
tooth	zobs (v)	[zɔbs]
lips	lūpas (s dsk)	[lu:pas]
chin	zods (v)	[zɔds]

ear	auss (s)	[aus]
neck	kakls (v)	[kakls]
eye	acs (s)	[ats]
pupil	acs zīlīte (s)	[ats zi:li:te]
eyebrow	uzacs (s)	[uzats]
eyelash	skropsta (s)	[skrɔpsta]

hair	mati (v dsk)	[mati]
hairstyle	frizūra (s)	[frizu:ra]
mustache	ūsas (s dsk)	[u:sas]
beard	bārda (s)	[ba:rda]
to have (a beard, etc.)	ir	[ir]
bald (adj)	plikgalvains	[plikgalvains]

hand	delna (s)	[delna]
arm	roka (s)	[rɔka]
finger	pirksts (v)	[pirksts]
nail	nags (v)	[nags]
palm	plauksta (s)	[plauksta]

shoulder	augšdelms (v)	[augʃdelms]
leg	kāja (s)	[ka:ja]
knee	celis (v)	[tselis]
heel	papēdis (v)	[pape:dis]
back	mugura (s)	[mugura]

5. Clothing. Personal accessories

clothes	apģērbs (v)	[apdʲe:rbs]
coat (overcoat)	mētelis (v)	[mɛ:telis]
fur coat	kažoks (v)	[kaʒɔks]
jacket (e.g., leather ~)	jaka (s)	[jaka]
raincoat (trenchcoat, etc.)	apmetnis (v)	[apmetnis]

shirt (button shirt)	krekls (v)	[krekls]
pants	bikses (s dsk)	[bikses]
suit jacket	žakete (s)	[ʒakɛte]
suit	uzvalks (v)	[uzvalks]

dress (frock)	kleita (s)	[klɛita]
skirt	svārki (v dsk)	[sva:rki]
T-shirt	sporta krekls (v)	[spɔrta krekls]
bathrobe	halāts (v)	[xala:ts]
pajamas	pidžama (s)	[pidʒama]
workwear	darba apģērbs (v)	[darba apdʲe:rbs]

underwear	veļa (s)	[vɛlʲa]
socks	zeķes (s dsk)	[zɛtʲes]
bra	krūšturis (v)	[kru:ʃturis]
pantyhose	zeķubikses (s dsk)	[zɛtʲubikses]
stockings (thigh highs)	sieviešu zeķes (s dsk)	[siɛviɛʃu zɛtʲes]
bathing suit	peldkostīms (v)	[peldkɔsti:ms]

hat	cepure (s)	[tsɛpure]
footwear	apavi (v dsk)	[apavi]
boots (e.g., cowboy ~)	zābaki (v dsk)	[za:baki]
heel	papēdis (v)	[pape:dis]

| shoestring | aukla (s) | [aukla] |
| shoe polish | apavu krēms (v) | [apavu kre:ms] |

gloves	cimdi (v dsk)	[tsimdi]
mittens	dūraiņi (v dsk)	[du:raiɲi]
scarf (muffler)	šalle (s)	[ʃalle]
glasses (eyeglasses)	brilles (s dsk)	[brilles]
umbrella	lietussargs (v)	[liɛtusargs]

tie (necktie)	kaklasaite (s)	[kaklasaite]
handkerchief	kabatlakatiņš (v)	[kabatlakatiɲʃ]
comb	ķemme (s)	[tʲemme]
hairbrush	matu suka (s)	[matu suka]

buckle	sprādze (s)	[spra:dze]
belt	josta (s)	[jɔsta]
purse	somiņa (s)	[sɔmiɲa]

6. House. Apartment

apartment	dzīvoklis (v)	[dzi:vɔklis]
room	istaba (s)	[istaba]
bedroom	guļamistaba (s)	[gulʲamistaba]
dining room	ēdamistaba (s)	[ɛ:damistaba]

living room	viesistaba (s)	[viɛsistaba]
study (home office)	kabinets (v)	[kabinets]
entry room	priekštelpa (s)	[priɛkʃtelpa]
bathroom (room with a bath or shower)	vannas istaba (s)	[vannas istaba]

| half bath | tualete (s) | [tualɛte] |

vacuum cleaner	putekļu sūcējs (v)	[puteklʲu su:tse:js]
mop	birste (s)	[birste]
dust cloth	lupata (s)	[lupata]
short broom	slota (s)	[slɔta]
dustpan	liekšķere (s)	[liɛkʃtʲɛre]

furniture	mēbeles (s dsk)	[me:bɛles]
table	galds (v)	[galds]
chair	krēsls (v)	[kre:sls]
armchair	atpūtas krēsls (v)	[atpu:tas kre:sls]

mirror	spogulis (v)	[spɔgulis]
carpet	paklājs (v)	[pakla:js]
fireplace	kamīns (v)	[kami:ns]
drapes	aizkari (v dsk)	[aizkari]
table lamp	galda lampa (s)	[galda lampa]
chandelier	lustra (s)	[lustra]
kitchen	virtuve (s)	[virtuve]

gas stove (range)	gāzes plīts (v)	[ga:zes pli:ts]
electric stove	elektriskā plīts (v)	[ɛlektriska: pli:ts]
microwave oven	mikroviļņu krāsns (v)	[mikrɔviļɲu kra:sns]

refrigerator	ledusskapis (v)	[lɛduskapis]
freezer	saldētava (s)	[saldɛ:tava]
dishwasher	trauku mazgājamā mašīna (s)	[trauku mazga:jama: maʃi:na]
faucet	krāns (v)	[kra:ns]

meat grinder	gaļas mašīna (s)	[gaļas maʃi:na]
juicer	sulu spiede (s)	[sulu spiɛde]
toaster	tosters (v)	[tɔstɛrs]
mixer	mikseris (v)	[mikseris]

coffee machine	kafijas aparāts (v)	[kafijas apara:ts]
kettle	tējkanna (s)	[te:jkanna]
teapot	tējkanna (s)	[te:jkanna]

TV set	televizors (v)	[tɛlevizɔrs]
VCR (video recorder)	videomagnetofons (v)	[videɔmagnetɔfɔns]
iron (e.g., steam ~)	gludeklis (v)	[gludeklis]
telephone	tālrunis (v)	[ta:lrunis]

Printed in Great Britain
by Amazon